EASTERN BROWN SNAKE

by Rachel Rose

Minneapolis, Minnesota

Credits
Cover and title page, © Ken Griffiths/Shutterstock; 4–5 © Robert Valentic/Minden; 6, © bgblue/iStock; 7, © Ken Griffiths/iStock; 8–9, © Ken Griffiths/iStock; 9, © RooM the Agency/Alamy; 11, © Doug Steley A/Alamy; 12–13, © Matt/Creative Commons Attribution 2.0 Generic; 15, © Ken Griffiths/iStock; 16, © iainesmith/iStock; 17, © Eight Ball Imagery/iStock; 18–19, © Helene Ecker/Animals Animals; 20–21, © Robert Valentic/Minden; 22, © Ken Griffiths/iStock; Throughout, © Stillfx/Adobe Stock.

Bearport Publishing Company Product Development Team
President: Jen Jenson; Director of Product Development: Spencer Brinker; Managing Editor: Allison Juda; Associate Editor: Naomi Reich; Associate Editor: Tiana Tran; Art Director: Colin O'Dea; Designer: Elena Klinkner; Designer: Kayla Eggert; Product Development Assistant: Owen Hamlin

STATEMENT ON USAGE OF GENERATIVE ARTIFICIAL INTELLIGENCE
Bearport Publishing remains committed to publishing high-quality nonfiction books. Therefore, we restrict the use of generative AI to ensure accuracy of all text and visual components pertaining to a book's subject. See BearportPublishing.com for details.

Library of Congress Cataloging-in-Publication Data

Names: Rose, Rachel, 1968- author.
Title: Eastern brown snake / by Rachel Rose.
Description: Minneapolis, Minnesota : Bearport Publishing Company, [2024] | Series: Danger down under | Includes bibliographical references and index.
Identifiers: LCCN 2023031106 (print) | LCCN 2023031107 (ebook) | ISBN 9798889164951 (library binding) | ISBN 9798889165026 (paperback) | ISBN 9798889165088 (ebook)
Subjects: LCSH: Snakes--Juvenile literature.
Classification: LCC QL666.O6 R56 2024 (print) | LCC QL666.O6 (ebook) | DDC 597.96--dc23/eng/20230713
LC record available at https://lccn.loc.gov/2023031106
LC ebook record available at https://lccn.loc.gov/2023031107

Copyright © 2024 Bearport Publishing Company. All rights reserved. No part of this publication may be reproduced in whole or in part, stored in any retrieval system, or transmitted in any form or by any means, electronic, mechanical, photocopying, recording, or otherwise, without written permission from the publisher.

For more information, write to Bearport Publishing, 5357 Penn Avenue South, Minneapolis, MN 55419.

CONTENTS

Deadly Danger 4
Sun-Lovin' Snake 6
Go Long 8
Eye Spy 10
Toxic Teeth 12
Step away from the Snake 14
The Hunter, Hunted 16
Mating, with a Twist 18
Small but Deadly 20

More about Eastern Brown Snakes 22
Glossary 23
Index 24
Read More 24
Learn More Online 24
About the Author 24

DEADLY DANGER

There's danger Down Under!

A **slender**, brown snake moves with lightning speed, catching a mouse and wrapping it up tightly. The mouse doesn't stand a chance as the eastern brown snake sinks its fangs into the **rodent**. Deadly **venom** spreads, and soon the Australian snake has its meal.

Despite having a deadly bite, the eastern brown snake's fangs are small compared to those of other snakes.

SUN-LOVIN' SNAKE

These deadly snakes live in eastern Australia, which is how they got their name. They can be spotted slithering through many kinds of **habitats**, but they are most frequently found in open grasslands and farmlands. Here, eastern brown snakes can soak up plenty of sunshine. These snakes love the heat.

! People living in Australia often call these **reptiles** common brown snakes.

Go Long

Eastern brown snakes are usually a shade of brown or gray. They have pale undersides, often dotted with pinkish-orange, brown, or gray spots.

These skinny snakes can grow about 7 feet (2.1 m) long. That's about the height of an average professional basketball player. But you wouldn't want to play ball with an eastern brown snake.

The eastern brown snake has hundreds of smooth, slightly glossy scales covering its body.

EYE SPY

These Australian reptiles have excellent vision, which they use to spy **prey**. What are the eastern brown snakes on the lookout for? They eat mostly rodents, which is why they often live in farmland areas where there are plenty of rats and mice. The snakes also chow down on frogs, small birds, and other reptiles.

! Many other kinds of snakes use smell to hunt, but that is not the primary sense eastern brown snakes use.

TOXIC TEETH

Once an eastern brown snake spots its next meal, the speedy snake catches the critter, squeezes, and bites. Powerful venom quickly spreads from its fangs.

Eastern brown snakes are some of the deadliest snakes in the world. Their venom is so toxic it doesn't take much to kill their prey.

! The eastern brown snake can move up to 12 miles per hour (19 kph).

An eastern brown snake making a meal of an eastern blue-tongued lizard

STEP AWAY FROM THE SNAKE

While some people have been bitten by these deadly snakes, it happens very rarely. Snakes usually save their venom for prey. Eastern brown snakes often hide or slither away when they come across humans. However, if they are caught by surprise, the snakes will rise up tall and open their mouths. That's a warning. The snake will attack if **provoked**.

!
The best thing to do if you come across a snake is to back away and let it move away from you.

THE HUNTER, HUNTED

On the flip side, humans can be dangerous to eastern brown snakes. These snakes are sometimes hunted by farmers and landowners who are worried about running into the dangerous creatures. Even more are run over by cars.

Some animals hunt eastern brown snakes, too. The snakes need to watch out for **feral** cats and birds of prey, such as eagles and hawks.

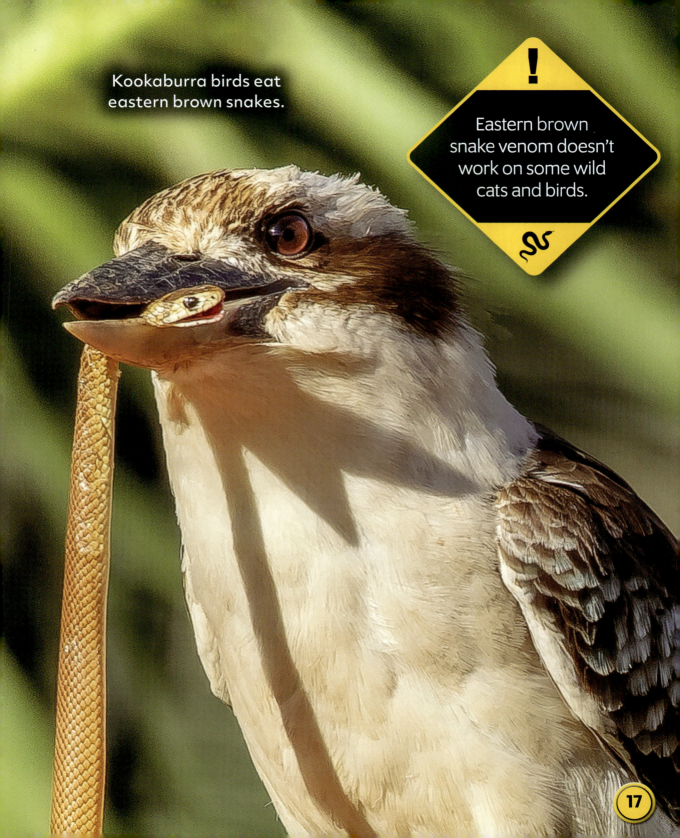

Kookaburra birds eat eastern brown snakes.

! Eastern brown snake venom doesn't work on some wild cats and birds.

MATING, WITH A TWIST

Eastern brown snakes typically live alone, but in late spring they come together to **mate**. In order to win over **female** partners, **male** brown snakes wrestle. The two males wind their bodies around each other, trying to overpower the other snake. It can take half an hour or more for one snake to come out on top.

!

Mating season for these Australian snakes is from about October until January.

SMALL BUT DEADLY

Female eastern brown snakes lay between 15 and 35 eggs at a time. It can take up to 90 days for the eggs to hatch.

Newborn baby snakes are called snakelets. Although only about 10 inches (25 cm) long, they aren't helpless. The babies' fangs are already full of venom. These snakelets are ready to take on the wild world Down Under!

> ! When they are about two years old, young eastern brown snakes are ready to start having babies of their own.

MORE ABOUT EASTERN BROWN SNAKES

⚠ Even though there aren't many deaths from snake bites in Australia, the eastern brown snake is responsible for more than half of them.

⚠ If given quickly enough, eastern brown snake **antivenom** can save people who have been bitten.

⚠ The eastern brown snake will hide in animal burrows or under logs or rocks.

⚠ These snakes can also use their tongues to tell when prey is around. They flick their tongues in the air and use special sensors to find their next meal.

⚠ As eastern brown snakes get older, their venom gets more deadly.

⚠ Like many kinds of snakes, eastern brown snakes hibernate during the winter.

GLOSSARY

antivenom a medicine that blocks the effects of venom

female an eastern brown snake that can lay eggs

feral wild

habitats places in nature where animals are found

male an eastern brown snake that cannot lay eggs

mate to come together to have young

prey animals that are hunted and eaten by other animals

provoked threatened into attacking

reptiles cold-blooded animals with dry, scaly skin that use lungs to breathe

rodent a small mammal with long front teeth, such as a mouse or a rat

slender thin and often long

venom poison from a snake that is injected through fangs

Index

eggs 20
fangs 4–5
female 18, 20
food 10
habitats 6
hatch 20
humans 14, 16
male 18
mate 18
prey 10, 12, 14, 16, 22
scales 9
snakelet 20
venom 4, 12, 14, 17, 20, 22

Read More

Cunningham, Malta. *How Do Snakes Poop? (Crazy Animal Facts).* Mankato, MN: Capstone Press, 2019.

Huddleston, Emma. *How Snakes Slither (The Science of Animal Movement).* Minneapolis: Abdo Publishing, 2021.

O'Daly, Anne. *Snakes (Animal Detectives).* Tucson, AZ: Brown Bear Books, 2020.

Learn More Online

1. Go to **www.factsurfer.com** or scan the QR code below.
2. Enter "**Eastern Brown Snake**" into the search box.
3. Click on the cover of this book to see a list of websites.

About the Author

Rachel Rose writes books for kids and teaches yoga. Her favorite animal of all is her dog, Sandy.